UNIVERSITY OF MINNESOTA

Richard Wright

BY ROBERT BONE

UNIVERSITY OF MINNESOTA PRESS • MINNEAPOLIS

Printed in the United States of America at
Jones Press, Minneapolis

Library of Congress Catalog Card Number: 77-625285

PUBLISHED IN GREAT BRITAIN, INDIA, AND PAKISTAN BY THE OXFORD
UNIVERSITY PRESS, LONDON, BOMBAY, AND KARACHI, AND IN CANADA
BY THE COPP CLARK PUBLISHING CO. LIMITED, TORONTO

RICHARD WRIGHT

ROBERT BONE is a professor of English at Teachers College, Columbia University. He is the author of the book *The Negro Novel in America*.

↗ *Richard Wright*

Richard Wright was born in 1908 on a cotton planta-
tion not far from Natchez, Mississippi. His father was a share-
cropper, a man of casual affections who deserted wife and family
when Wright was only five. His mother struggled ineffectively as
cook or housemaid to raise two growing boys. When Wright was
ten or twelve she suffered a series of paralytic strokes. Her chronic
illness set the emotional tone of his life and imbued his writing
with a somber cast. Anguish is Wright's characteristic note; four
of his epigraphs are taken from the Book of Job.

Hunger and violence were his family heirlooms. A hunger
that dominates his childhood memories; that aroused a deep, bio-
logical bitterness; that drew him to the ranks of the Communist
party, and left him with an enduring sympathy for the dispos-
sessed. And a violence, inflicted by his immediate family, but
stemming from the larger violence of southern life. Surrounded
by a latent terror, which might be called forth by any act of self-
assertion, the Negro family tried to beat the dangerous assertive-
ness out of its wayward members. Never lacking in waywardness,
Wright was severely beaten, his spirit branded with the images
of violence that crowd the pages of his fiction.

Wright's rebellious tendencies were reinforced by an early
exposure to Seventh-Day Adventism. His grandmother's house-
hold, where he spent a crucial portion of his childhood, was
pervaded by a stern evangelism. Half a dozen daily prayers were
supplemented by all-night revival meetings. Dietary restrictions
further reduced an already meager food supply. Boyish recrea-
tions such as baseball and marbles were forbidden. Books on

nonreligious subjects were proscribed as "the Devil's work." This pious woman, in short, tried by every stratagem to save her grandson from the world. Wright's response, in his mature years, was to embrace a humanist philosophy, militantly secular and implacably hostile to any brand of otherworldliness.

Wright's boyhood was too turbulent to permit of much formal schooling. Shunted back and forth among his mother's relatives, moving constantly from one southern town to the next, he was seldom able to complete a year of unbroken study. At the age of sixteen he graduated from the ninth grade, without having undertaken anything that might be called a high-school education. This lack of formal study, which Wright shares with an earlier generation of American naturalists, cannot be ignored in any just appraisal of his work. If it compels a tribute to his raw power, it explains a persistent awkwardness that mars all but his finest efforts.

Against heavy odds, and on rations as slender as his daily plate of greens, Wright's imagination flickered into life. Sunday supplements, cheap pulp tales, and vivid country sermons fed the flame. During an enforced hour of prayer the lonely boy amused himself by writing poetry and fiction. At the age of fifteen he published a story in the local Negro press. Such ambitions in a black boy were a challenge and affront to the southern way of life. In them may be found the seeds of Wright's conflict with the white South.

Richard Wright grew to manhood in the afterglow of human slavery. A generation from absolute power, the whites were determined to restore their traditional prerogatives. A generation from the auction block, the blacks clung for protection to their ancient, servile ways. Wright wanted no part of this accommodation. His insistence on behaving like a man, his stubborn refusal to know his place, and above all his expanding sensibility brought him into deadly conflict with the closed society. Knowing that his life depended on it, in his seventeenth year he fled to Memphis, Tennessee, the first stop on his northern journey.

It was in Memphis that his intellectual awakening occurred. Having read in the local press an editorial attacking H. L. Mencken, he resolved to examine for himself the writings of a man who could so enrage the southern whites. Barred from access to the public library, he finessed the Jim Crow laws by forging a note: "Dear Madam: Will you please let this nigger boy have some books by H. L. Mencken?" Mencken's essays were the gateway to a new world. What appealed to Wright was the man's irreverence, his open mockery of human and divine authority. Mencken was his introduction to the modern temper; his link to the muckraking spirit and the naturalist tradition; his preparation for the fiction of Sinclair Lewis, Theodore Dreiser, and Stephen Crane.

In the winter of 1927 Wright and his family migrated to Chicago, the city where he was to pass the next decade of his life. For several hard-pressed years he worked as porter, dishwasher, part-time postal clerk, life-insurance salesman. During the depression he suffered the humiliations of unemployment and relief. At one point a relief agency placed him in the South Side Boys' Club, where he met the living models from whom he was to sketch Bigger Thomas. In the end he found a refuge, like many writers of his generation, preparing guidebooks for the Federal Writers' Project.

Chicago captured Wright's imagination. He responded to its massive scale and quickened tempo, its toughness, vitality, and raw beauty. A newcomer to the urban scene, he sought to understand the social transformation in which he was caught up, to gain perspective on his life experience. He turned at first to social science: "The huge mountains of fact piled up by the Department of Sociology at the University of Chicago gave me my first concrete vision of the forces that molded the urban Negro's body and soul."

Social science became a permanent feature of Wright's world view. From the work of Robert Park, Robert Redfield, and Louis Wirth, he absorbed the concepts of industrialization, secularization, urbanization, and social class. From Horace Cayton he absorbed the social science ethos, with its emphasis on field study, statistical methods, and empirical research. Wright acknowledges his debt to the social sciences in his introduction to *Black Metropolis,* a monumental study of the South Side ghetto by Cayton and St. Clair Drake.

Wright's second attempt to achieve perspective led him to contemplate the October Revolution. Had the Bolsheviks not organized an inert peasant mass into an effective instrument of social change? Were they not transforming a static, tradition-bound, and absolutist feudal order — not unlike rural Mississippi — into a modern industrial society? And was the capitalist order not visibly disintegrating in 1932? A revolutionary movement that promised to organize the outcast and rejected; that provided outlets for rebelliousness and thwarted self-expression; that countered loneliness with fraternity, and self-hatred with a universal vision: this was irresistible.

Wright joined the Communist party in 1932 and maintained his membership for twelve years. In Chicago he was executive secretary of the local John Reed Club and an activist in his South Side party cell. In New York he was Harlem editor of the *Daily Worker,* a member of the executive board of the League of American Writers, and a vice-president of American Peace Mobilization. At the same time, inclined by nature to a crusty individualism, he chafed under party discipline, resented interference with his writing, and was repelled by the atmosphere of

8

paranoia that prevailed during the Stalin era. These disaffections led to his expulsion in 1944.

Richard Wright served his literary apprenticeship under the tutelage of the Communist party. As a member of the John Reed Club, he contributed poetry and fiction to *Left Front, Anvil,* and *New Masses.* As a party activist, he acquired a variety of journalistic and editorial skills. His party contacts, moreover, were a source of material for his first book. In his South Side unit Wright met a Negro Communist whose early life in Mississippi inspired him to attempt a series of novellas. These stories won first prize in a competition among WPA writers. They were published in 1938 under the title *Uncle Tom's Children.*

Wright moved from Chicago to New York in 1937. Ten years later, he became a permanent expatriate in Paris. During most of the intervening decade he lived in Brooklyn or in Greenwich Village. These were the years of Wright's most enduring literary work. They witnessed the publication of his first four books and the establishment of his worldwide reputation. They were also the years of an ill-fated first marriage, and of an enduring union with Ellen Poplar, a Brooklyn girl of Jewish antecedents. Two daughters were born of this union.

New York did not engage the deepest layers of Wright's imagination. It is at most, in his later fiction, a thinly painted backdrop for some drama of the soul. The city served him rather as a vantage point from which to view the past. These were retrospective years, in which Wright attempted to assimilate the traumas of his youth and early manhood and impose on this material a literary form. He became, in the process, consciously concerned with matters of technique. Searching for clues among the masters, he ransacked the letters of Dostoevski, the prefaces of Conrad and of Henry James. His reward was the triumph of his first novel.

9

Published in the spring of 1940, *Native Son* was an instantaneous success. A best seller and Book-of-the-Month Club selection, it was subsequently adapted for the stage by Orson Welles and for the cinema by Wright himself. After years of personal hardship Wright's career was launched: serious attention, financial independence, and professional status were assured. At the same time, *Native Son* was a major breakthrough for the Negro writer. With one powerful thrust, Wright had breached the ghetto walls. He had gained a hearing, claimed a territory, challenged the conscience of a nation. In recognition of this achievement, he was awarded the coveted Spingarn Medal by the National Association for the Advancement of Colored People.

Wright's third book, *Twelve Million Black Voices*, appeared in 1941. Conceived as a folk history of the American Negro, the book consists of photographs by Edwin Rosskam and a text by Richard Wright. This was followed in 1945 by *Black Boy*, whose sales exceeded even those of *Native Son*. It is Wright's best book. By virtue of its depth of feeling, its sustained dramatic power, its relentless unmasking of the self, and still more naked exposure of the social order, *Black Boy* is an American classic.

Black Boy was followed by a long period of public silence. It was a time of introspection, of honest effort to replace the god that failed. When Wright resumed his career in the 1950's he was working in a different vein. But the Richard Wright of *Native Son* and *Black Boy* had become a culture hero. He inspired a host of imitators, both novelists and poets, who flourished in the postwar years. No Negro writer was entirely immune from Wright's influence. Even the most original of his contemporaries were forced to reckon with his presence and somehow circumvent it, in order to protect their own careers.

Some months after the liberation of Paris, Gertrude Stein published an account of the Nazi occupation called *Wars I Have*

Seen. The book was reviewed by Richard Wright in the pages of *PM*. Pleased by the review, Miss Stein initiated a correspondence, in the course of which Wright expressed a desire to visit France. The upshot was a formal invitation, issued by the French government over the signatures of France's most distinguished men of letters. In the spring of 1946, when the Wrights arrived in Paris, Gertrude Stein helped them to arrange for housing and introduced them to her circle of Parisian friends.

In spite of a growing affection for Paris, the Wrights did not decide at once to emigrate. After a pleasant sojourn of six months they returned to New York with every intention of resuming their accustomed lives. They had not reckoned with the strength of Wright's expatriate impulse. He embarked once more for Paris in the summer of 1947 and remained until his death in 1960. His principal residence, during these final years of exile, was a spacious apartment in the rue Monsieur le Prince, adjacent to the Jardin du Luxembourg. In 1956 he bought a country house in Normandy, near the village of Ailly, where he retired to write, or, confessing to his friends that he was still a country boy, to grow potatoes, corn, and collard greens.

Throughout his Paris years Wright enjoyed the status of an *homme célèbre*. He was invited to lecture in the major European capitals, was widely quoted in the press, and made frequent guest appearances on radio and television. His private life was invaded by a constant stream of visitors to his Left Bank apartment. African diplomats, Parisian intellectuals, eminent American Negroes, writers of international repute, luminaries of the democratic left, were among his honored guests. Foremost among these personages, in terms of their influence on Wright's work, was the group of French existentialists which included Jean-Paul Sartre and Simone de Beauvoir.

What attracted Wright to existentialism was its tendency to

make a virtue out of rootlessness, to conceive of the human condition as a kind of cosmic exile. Himself an exile, twice removed from Mississippi soil, he responded by exulting in his fate, by glorifying heroes who are cut off from the past and dependent on the self alone. Wright explores these themes in three novels: *The Outsider* (1953), *Savage Holiday* (1954), and *The Long Dream* (1958). The novels are intended as a celebration of the rootlessness of modern man. Unhappily, for reasons that have everything to do with rootlessness, the fiction of the fifties is a travesty of Wright's best work.

Meanwhile, in the decade following World War II, a series of colonial wars and revolutions shook the foundations of European empire. With the defeat or withdrawal of imperialist power, nation after new nation emerged in Africa and Asia. Fascinated by this confrontation of a civilization and its former subject peoples, Wright determined to witness it at first hand. He traveled to Ghana in 1953, to Indonesia in 1955, and, by way of contrast, to Spain in 1954. Each journey produced a book: *Black Power* (1954), *The Color Curtain* (1956), and *Pagan Spain* (1957). To these must be added *White Man, Listen!* (1957), a summary statement of Wright's concern with the colonial revolution.

Richard Wright died of a heart attack in 1960 at the age of fifty-two. He had published eleven books in the course of a short lifetime. Two more were brought out by the Wright estate. One of these, *Lawd Today* (1963), adds nothing to his reputation. It is an apprentice novel, written during his Chicago years and dealing with the sordid milieu of a Negro postal clerk. The other, *Eight Men* (1961), is a collection of short stories, written at various stages of Wright's career. Uneven, badly edited, and containing only two unpublished stories, the book does serve to rescue from oblivion some of Wright's most impressive fiction.

The life of Richard Wright unfolded in progressive stages. Mississippi, Chicago, New York, Paris: these were the milestones of a picaresque journey. Moving instinctively toward greater freedom, wider horizons, more cosmopolitan perspectives, Wright attempted to transcend the narrow and the local, the pinched and straitened outlook of the tribal soul. His life was a persistent quest for meaning: of the South, of industrial America, ultimately of the Western world. To share with others a liberating knowledge of the white man's ways is the motivating force of his career. To this end he invades the silent places of the human heart and bruits his discoveries to the world.

We turn now to the tasks of literary criticism: the exposition of principal themes and the evaluation of individual works. Richard Wright's output is readily divided into two periods. The first encompasses the writing done in the United States, roughly from 1935 to 1945; the second, the writing done in France, roughly from 1950 to 1960. These two productive decades, separated by a period of personal and political crisis, are quite distinct in subject matter and philosophic ambience.

Wright's early subject is the Great Migration: that vast demographic shift of the Negro population from rural South to urban North. His most explicit treatment of the subject is the documentary study *Twelve Million Black Voices*. This book, which remains a useful summary of Negro folk experience, forms the programmatic basis of Wright's American period. Thus *Uncle Tom's Children* and *Black Boy* are set in rural Mississippi. They deal with the conditions of injustice and oppression which motivate the Great Migration. *Lawd Today* and *Native Son* are set in metropolitan Chicago and are concerned with the Negro migrant's adjustment to the urban scene.

From a literary point of view, which of Wright's early works are likely to endure? Surely *Black Boy*, his solid contribution to

13

the art of autobiography. Surely *Native Son*, his most successful full-length novel. And surely "The Man Who Lived Underground," that remarkable novella which explores the innermost recesses of the black man's soul. It is to these three works that we must turn to discover the central thrust of Wright's imagination.

Black Boy forces us, in the first instance, to imagine southern life from a Negro point of view. What we discover from this harrowing perspective is that the entire society is mobilized to keep the Negro in his place: to restrict his freedom of movement, discourage his ambition, and banish him forever to the nether regions of subordination and inferiority. This attempt to mark off in advance the boundaries of human life is Wright's essential theme. "The white South said that I had a 'place' in life. Well, I had never felt my 'place'; or, rather, my deepest instincts had always made me reject the 'place' to which the white South had assigned me."

The spiritual deprivations suffered under such a system are embedded in the language of the book. Wright describes himself as trapped, imprisoned, stifled, stunted, curbed, condemned. At the most elementary levels of human existence he is forbidden to touch, to look, to speak, to eat, to play, to read, to be curious, to dream, aspire, expand, or grow. Ringed about with prohibitions and taboos, he is denied access to experience, the catalyst of spiritual growth. Assigned by tradition to a demeaning role, he is deprived of possibility, of what he might become. Defined by others, and manipulated by means of these twisted definitions, he is robbed of personality, identity, a sense of self.

Wright's response to the straitened circumstances of his life was implacable rebellion. The more his society insisted on setting artificial bounds to his experience, the greater his compulsion to trespass, to taste forbidden fruit. The more his society conspired against his human weight and presence, the more determined he became to assert himself, to compel the recognition of his individuality. Hence his urge to write, which was born of a fierce desire to affirm his own reality. What obsessed him was a fear of nothingness, of becoming in the end what the white South proclaimed him to be: a non-man.

The linguistic equivalent of nothingness is silence. Throughout *Black Boy* we can observe Wright's obsessive fear of speechlessness: "I was frightened speechless"; "I wanted to speak, but I could not move my tongue." Southern Negroes are forced to accommodate their speech habits to the expectations of the whites. To be "sassy," after all, is to be *outspoken*. But Wright could never master the language of self-effacement. His career as a writer was in fact a rejoinder to the repression of Negro speech. To speak out at all costs; to refuse to be intimidated into silence: this is the force behind the stridency and clamor of his prose.

Wright's literary aspirations were profoundly subversive of his social order. "My environment," he observes, "contained nothing more alien than writing or the desire to express one's self in writing." Nor was this a matter primarily of race. In traditional societies, sensibility itself is regarded with suspicion. Truth and wisdom are thought to be transmitted from the past, rather than discovered by the exploring self. *Black Boy* may thus be read as a drama of sensibility, in which the individual perceptions of the artist-hero are pitted against the inherited codes and a priori judgments of a closed society.

A closed society and a quest for self-realization: these are the preconditions of the picaresque. The form appeared in European letters toward the end of the feudal and beginning of the bourgeois epoch. It reflects the breakdown of static social relations and their replacement by more fluid forms. The picaresque tradition, with its thrust toward a greater personal and social freedom, is readily adapted to the needs of the black writer.

The picaresque hero is a rootless man, a wanderer. No longer an organic part of a stable social order, he undertakes a symbolic journey, whose aim is the emancipation of the self. On the open road, he has a series of adventures which test his capacity for improvisation. Living by his wits, he often employs questionable methods. If he is something of a rogue and mischief maker, it is because his energies cannot be absorbed within the legal order. His society is closed against him; it drives him out; it threatens him with spiritual death. To survive he becomes a hustler, a confidence man, an outlaw, a criminal.

Black Boy conforms in all essentials to the pattern of the picaresque. The book consists of a series of encounters with the closed society which lead to an overwhelming conclusion: flight. The last five chapters are devoted to the early stages of the author's northern journey. This symbolic journey, moreover, is crime-tinged. In order to finance his flight to Memphis, Wright turns to petty crime. He begins by selling bootleg liquor to white prostitutes, proceeds to a complicated ticket swindle at a local movie house, and ends by stealing cans of fruit preserves from the commissary of a Negro college.

Wright insists upon his criminality, for it reveals the hidden meaning of his life. At the same time, he insists on his essential innocence. The explanation of this paradox lies in the domain of the picaresque. What motivates the rogue-hero, what pushes him beyond the pale, is a disillusioning encounter with *legal wrong*: "I had now seen at close quarters the haughty white men who made the laws; I had seen how they acted, how they regarded black people, how they regarded me; and I no longer felt bound by the laws which black and white were supposed to obey in common. I was outside those laws; the white people had told me so."

This sense of being outside or above the law is characteristic

16

of Wright's fictional heroes. Typically they are innocent outlaws, ethical criminals, who murder with a deep conviction of their own blamelessness. Despite the horror of their crimes, they can never muster a convincing show of remorse. In effect, Wright claims immunity from ordinary standards of justice and morality. Whatever the philosophical validity of such a claim, its emotional source is plainly Wright's experience as a Negro in the deep South. The ultimate crime, for which he cannot bring himself to acknowledge any guilt, but for which he knows that he will nonetheless be punished, is the crime of being black.

The secondary theme of *Black Boy* is Wright's emphatic rejection of southern Negro values. A stubborn individualism was the basis of this conflict. For the ethos of the black South, conditioned by generations of slavery, was pre-individualistic. Instinctively the black community sought to suppress individuality, discourage competition, and restrain aggressiveness. Insofar as the black South opposed his efforts at self-realization, Wright did not hesitate to attack its value system. Like Huck Finn, who fled as much from Pap as from the Widow Douglas, he was forced to number his own kin among his enemies.

Wright's estrangement from communal values can be traced to his affiliation with Seventh-Day Adventism. To keep the Sabbath on Saturday, after all, is a deeply divisive ritual in a community of Methodists and Baptists. When his mother, hoping to reduce the boy's sense of being different, brought him to a Methodist Sunday school, it was already too late: "I had been kept out of their world too long ever to be able to become a real part of it." This sense of not belonging would persist throughout Wright's career. He remained an outsider, a solitary artist whose supreme value was not the welfare of the group but the realization of the self.

Of all the communal rituals demanded of a Negro adolescent,

none was more compelling than church membership. This was the supreme test of racial loyalty: "We young men had been trapped by the community, the tribe in which we lived and of which we were a part. The tribe, for its own safety, was asking us to be at one with it." Wright would never give the sign of allegiance. With all his being he resisted the tribal spirit. A certain independence and aloofness, a firm rejection of nationalism and negritude, an insistence on broader loyalties than race, would be characteristic of his life and art.

What alienated Wright above all from the black community was the southern Negro's complicity in his own abasement. Thus the boy's symbolic confrontation with his Uncle Tom, who undertakes to teach him with a hickory switch "to grin, hang my head, and mumble apologetically when I was spoken to." The Negro family, hoping to protect the child from violent reprisal, agrees to serve as a surrogate of the white power structure. To be an Uncle Tom, in short, is to enforce the white man's discipline against your own.

But still more shameful is the effort to enforce that discipline against the self; still more sinister the Uncle Tom within. Wright marvels at the willingness of southern Negroes to police themselves; to curb their natural impulses, their speech and gestures, aspirations, hopes, and dreams. Here is the ultimate betrayal: the collusion of the self in its own annihilation.

The archetype of self-annihilation is the Sambo figure, the Negro who approximates in his behavior the clownish role assigned him by the whites. This figure appears in *Black Boy* in the episode of Shorty, the elevator boy who invites a white man to kick him for a quarter. We shall encounter this symbolic clown elsewhere in the Wright canon, notably in *The Outsider*. For the moment it will suffice to recognize in Shorty a symbol of psychic nothingness. This is the inauthentic self that Wright

18

repudiates, the role that he would rather die than play, the void from which he flees in order to establish an identity.

Wright's response to the self-limiting tendencies in Negro life was a profound disgust. That disgust, so perilously close to self-hatred, was scarcely to be acknowledged by the conscious self. Yet it forms the basis, in Wright's fiction, for his uncomplimentary images of Negro life. On the intellectual plane, it leads him consistently to underestimate his Negro heritage. In a famous passage in *Black Boy*, too long to quote, he deplores the bleakness and barrenness of Negro culture. This mistaken judgment, which tempted him to flee rather than explore the Negro past, has had disastrous consequences for his art.

That art, at its most robust, is to be found in *Black Boy*. Most of Wright's work is seriously flawed, marred by a tendency to preach and editorialize. The long courtroom speech in *Native Son* is only the most regrettable instance of this fault. In *Black Boy*, however, Wright entrusts his meaning entirely to his images. The didactic tendency is suppressed, and the narrative element allowed to speak for itself. The result is writing of unusual imaginative force.

The artistic strength of *Black Boy* lies in its power to evoke the spiritual realities of southern Negro life by means of parable. The structure of the book, deriving from the tradition of the picaresque, consists of a series of dramatic episodes. Each episode, moreover, is parabolic: it comes to stand for something larger than itself. Thus we have parables of blasted hope, inauthentic selfhood, social stagnation, embattled individuality. Toward the end these parables coalesce into a single vision. They are seen to represent the options of the artist-hero. He must choose between the terrible alternatives of martyrdom or exile.

Black Boy is at bottom a parable of extrication. Its theme is the judgment and rejection of a narrow world. The nature of that world is hinted at in Wright's explicit tribute to H. L. Mencken. The American South, after all, is a part of the Bible Belt, a stronghold of rural fundamentalism. Like Mencken, Dreiser, Anderson, and Lewis, Wright felt compelled to disengage his sensibility from the stifling atmosphere of a provincial, puritanical, and philistine America. This is Wright's American tradition: the revolt from the village. That his village is southern rather than midwestern simply adds a racial dimension to a fundamental impulse toward cultural freedom.

Native Son appeared in 1940, five years in advance of *Black Boy*. Wright had not yet fully plumbed the meaning of his Mississippi youth, and the outlaw bent of his imagination had not yet found its proper form. Nonetheless, the pattern of the picaresque is plainly visible in *Native Son*. Here the closed society is the northern ghetto, but it is equally restrictive of Negro life. The symbolic journey is internalized: it is not so much geographical as spiritual or moral. Instead of flight from an oppressive social order we have an open foray into criminality.

Book I presents a northern version of the closed society. In a crucial episode Bigger Thomas and his gang are "playing white." To amuse themselves they assume the roles of generals, financial magnates, and government officials. Barred in real life from the military, industrial, or political hierarchies, their fantasy dwells on these forbidden roles. The limits and restrictions that push them toward a social marginality are deeply resented by Bigger and his friends: "We black and they white. They got things and we ain't. They do things and we can't. It's just like living in jail. Half the time I feel like I'm on the outside of the world peeping in through a knot-hole in the fence."

What is missing in Bigger's world is the element of exploit or heroic action. Yet if all legitimate outlets for exploit and adventure are closed to him, the black man will assert his claim to heroism through extralegal means. That is the symbolism of Bigger's name: he aspires to action on the epic plane; he seeks a challenge worthy of his manhood; he insists on something "bigger" than the cramped horizons of ghetto life. The central irony of *Native Son* is that he can find a larger and more meaningful existence only through violence and crime.

Bigger's murder of a white girl, Mary Dalton, is philosophical in motive. All his life he has been treated like a cipher, made to feel his nothingness. Reduced to a shadowy presence in the white man's mind, he has been drained of all substantiality. Bigger murders in order to become real, to make the white world acknowledge his existence. The whites conspire to ignore his human presence. Very well, then: let them ignore the presence of a white corpse! It is an act of metaphysical reprisal. If the white world *blots out* his reality, he will blot out the reality of the white world.

Book II develops Bigger as an outlaw hero. In the fiery crucible of crime he discovers a new sense of purpose and a new freedom of action. As a murderer he acquires a new conviction of his own worth, even his superiority. The people around him seem blinded by illusion, by conventional notions of reality, but Bigger has experienced a form of transcendence. He has moved beyond the law, beyond convention, beyond good and evil, and he is now able to see beyond the surfaces of things. His sudden release from the invisible forces that oppress him propels him toward a deeper vision of reality.

Bigger's heightened powers are displayed in the episode of the kidnap note. He emerges as a kind of artist, creating fictive worlds, inventing scenarios, manipulating others as he himself was formerly manipulated. He combines, in short, those qualities of creativity and illegality that are typical of the picaresque hero. For the creative impulse, denied legitimate expression, will seek an antisocial outlet. In Bigger's case, the result is an inspired criminality; in Wright's, a revolutionary art.

Book III is a quest for values. As Bigger faces death in the electric chair he seeks desperately for something to believe in, something that will give his life, and therefore death, a meaning. Traditional religious values no longer can sustain him. An old preacher visits Bigger's cell to comfort him. In praying for his soul he summons "images which had once given him a reason for living, had explained the world." But Bigger emphatically repudiates his ministry.

The visit of the old preacher is followed by that of the young Communist, Jan Erlone. Jan is the apostle of a secular religion, and together with the lawyer, Max, he represents an alternative to Christian values, a new evangelism capable of explaining the world. Jan and Max offer Bigger a vision of human fraternity from which no one is excluded on grounds of race. But Bigger rejects their vision as inauthentic, false to his experience. The political commitment that saved Wright from nothingness is not available to Bigger. He is thrown back on himself and what he has become.

The novel moves, in its denouement, toward values that we have learned to recognize as existentialist. Having rejected Christianity and Communism Bigger finds the strength to die in the courageous acceptance of his existential self: "What I killed for, I *am!*" In embracing his own murderous instincts, however, Wright's hero is compelled to sacrifice other and perhaps more basic values. He has established an identity through murder, but that identity, by virtue of its horror, has cut him off from the human community of which he longs to be a part. That is the meaning of Max's profound revulsion in the final scene.

The triumph of authenticity, in short, is offset by the defeat of love. For beneath Bigger's posture of defiance is a desperate craving to be loved. What he has hoped for all along from those who have rejected him is some gesture of affection, some mutual exchange if not of love at least of recognition. Now these hopes are doomed. In accepting the brand of Cain he confirms his outcast state. The novel thus concludes on an unresolved chord. Bigger achieves a partial affirmation, but only at the expense of his deepest needs.

As a work of art *Native Son* is seriously flawed. The first two books are solidly designed and fully realized, but in Book III Wright has allowed his statement as a Communist to overwhelm his statement as an artist. Plot dissolves into improbability as fictional events are manipulated to score propaganda points. Characterization descends to caricature, and Bigger alone persuades us of his authenticity. Stylistically there is a sharp decline, all the more surprising after the sure control of Books I and II. Capping these disasters is the long speech of Bigger's lawyer, who is at once a mouthpiece for the author and a spokesman for the party line.

Beyond the obvious flaws of agitprop there is a philosophical confusion at the heart of *Native Son*. As a naturalist, an amateur social scientist, and a Communist, Wright is committed to the concept of determinism. His approach to Bigger's crime, for example, is environmentalist: "Men like you made him what he is." That is the entire burden of the lawyer's speech, and its purpose is to minimize the element of choice in Bigger's criminal behavior. It is a question of conditioning, of automatic reflexes. Bigger's actions are presented as inevitable, compulsive, beyond conscious control, or, in a word, unfree.

At the same time Wright is moving toward a concept of existential freedom. As we have seen, the picaresque hero journeys toward the realm of possibility, and away from the tyranny of predetermined forms. The object of his quest is an unprecedented freedom of action, though he turn outlaw to achieve it. Thus with Wright's hero, who attains the desired degree of indeterminacy through murder: "Bigger had murdered and created a new life for himself." Such a concept must bring into play the elements of decision, purpose, choice, and moral agency. The emphasis is on the creative act, which by definition cannot be unfree.

The language of the novel reflects the author's philosophical confusion. For each of his perspectives Wright employs a distinct rhetorical style. On occasion the two rhetorics collide: "The actions that resulted in the death of those two women were as instinctive and inevitable as breathing or blinking one's eyes. It was an act of *creation!*" But murder is either inevitable or creative. Only by a conjuring trick, by a rigorous separation of Bigger No. 1 from Bigger No. 2 can Wright maintain the semblance of novelistic unity.

Two philosophical perspectives and two literary traditions meet and clash in *Native Son*. The one stems from Dreiser, and more precisely *An American Tragedy*; the other from Dostoevski, and particularly *Crime and Punishment*. Dreiser appealed to Wright's rationalist side; Dostoevski to his demonic urges. At this stage of his career he was under the illusion that Clyde Griffiths and Raskolnikov could be incorporated in a single hero. Increasingly the Dreiserian strain in Wright gave way to the Dostoevskian. After his break with the party, and hence with socialist realism, he was free to follow the demonic promptings of his deepest nature.

Despite its serious shortcomings *Native Son* must be counted among the major American novels. If the function of the literary imagination is to conquer new frontiers, to prepare unpopulated regions of the soul for permanent settlement, then Wright must be honored for his pioneering role. He has shown us a nation divided against itself; a gulf so vast between the white suburb and the black ghetto that no kindly paternalism can span it. He has revealed the hatred and resentment of the ghetto masses and exposed a psychic wound so deep that only violence can cauterize it. He has given us, in short, the first authentic portrait of the stranger in our midst.

Urban nihilism is the real subject of *Native Son*. Wright confronts us with a segment of the nation that believes in nothing. His hero, in the last analysis, can affirm no values other than his own acts of violence. Bigger Thomas now is legion, and his nihilism threatens not only the tranquillity but the very foundations of the republic. This is the substance of Wright's prophetic vision. We have spawned in the city slums a breed of men who are radically alienated from the dominant values of their culture. And this rough beast, its hour come round at last, slouches toward the ghettoes to be born.

At the height of his artistic powers, between the publication of *Native Son* and *Black Boy*, Wright conceived and executed his most flawless work of fiction. "The Man Who Lived Underground" is a minor masterpiece, deserving of an honored place in American literary history. An early version of the story appeared in *Accent* (Spring 1942); an enlarged version in Edwin Seaver's *Cross-Section* (1944). The finished product, a novella of some fifty pages, may most conveniently be found in the posthumous collection of Wright's shorter fiction, *Eight Men*.

The image of the Negro as underground man had its origin in Wright's personal experience. During the winter of 1932, he was employed by a Chicago hospital to look after the experimental animals. He and his fellow porters were confined to the basement corridors of the institution, restricted to what might be called an underground point of view: "The hospital kept us four Negroes as though we were close kin to the animals we tended, huddled together down in the underworld corridors of the hospital, separated by a vast psychological distance from the significant processes of the rest of the hospital — just as America had kept us locked in the dark underworld of American life for three hundred years. . . ."

This germinal idea was subsequently deepened and enriched through Wright's discovery of *Notes from Underground*. In the Dostoevski novella he encountered a familiar state of soul, a spiritual plight bearing an uncanny resemblance to that of the American Negro. For Dostoevski's hero is a man of morbid sensitivity who feels himself to be rejected by the world. Convinced that he excites aversion, he broods on his humiliations and harbors violent fantasies of revenge. He is a man possessed by the demons of shame, self-hatred, and vindictiveness. The negative quality of his existence is symbolized by his withdrawal to an underground den.

Wright's subterranean world is a symbol of the Negro's social marginality. Thrust from the upperworld by the racial exclusiveness of whites, he is forced to lead an underground existence. Wright was groping for a spatial metaphor that would render the Negro's ambiguous relationship to Western culture. In *Native Son*, seeking to express the same reality, he hit upon the metaphor of No Man's Land. It conjures up a bleak and sterile landscape in which a hapless soldier crouches, in constant danger of annihilation by enemy or friend. Some of the same qualities of desolation, abandonment, and vulnerability will be found in the bizarre world of Wright's underground hero.

"The Man Who Lived Underground" is a variation on the theme of nihilism. To be driven underground is to suffer spiritual death, to be the victim of metaphysical annihilation. The social reality here expressed has to do with anti-Negro stereotypes. For the stereotype, which is a projection of the white man's mind, drains the Negro of reality. It draws attention to itself, and away from the black man's humanity. What is left him is a shadow-world, an underground existence in some murky region of the white man's soul. A fear of nothingness is thus the key to Negro personality.

At the bottom of the Negro's metaphysical dread is his fear of rejection. This is the emotional core of Richard Wright's art. Whether we recall that his own mother beat him half to death at the age of four, or focus on the racial traumas of his later years, it is evident that this excruciating pain is his chief preoccupation. Wright's essential contribution as an artist is his understanding of the link between emotional rejection and philosophic nothingness. He is indebted for this insight to the work of William James, whose devoted reader he remained throughout his adult life.

In his introduction to *Black Metropolis* Wright quotes a crucial passage from William James: "No more fiendish punishment could be devised . . . than that one should be turned loose in society and remain absolutely unnoticed by all the members thereof. If no one turned round when we entered, answered when we spoke, or minded what we did, but if every person we met 'cut us dead,' and acted as if we were non-existent things, a kind of rage and impotent despair would ere long well up in us, from which the cruelest bodily tortures would be a relief; for these would make us feel that, however bad might be our plight, we had not sunk to such a depth as to be unworthy of attention at all."

It is the pain so vividly conveyed by James that we must seek to understand. Wright's entire career may be regarded as a search for ways of dealing with this pain. He comes closest to realizing his essential theme in "The Man Who Lived Underground." Here the fabulous plot and surrealistic style serve as a kind of mask or veil, drawn over the nakedness, the raw and quivering wounds of the Negro psyche. We are dealing with veiled confession, with experiences too painful to approach directly, with meanings that can only be expressed in symbolic language. The novella confronts us with underground (i.e., repressed) material. It can only be retrieved by a strenuous effort of imagination.

Wright's fable is best conveyed through a series of images. We begin with a Negro fugitive, running from the police. He dodges down a manhole and finds himself in the municipal sewer system. Now a sewer is a place for discarded and rejected things, a place of filth and excrement, bad odors, revulsion and disgust. Wright employs it as a symbol of Negro life. For white people shrink from the black man as if he were a filthy thing. They respond to his dark skin as if it were dirty. He is made to feel repulsive, and Wright's sewer is a brilliant projection of this feeling.

The fugitive explores the sewer until he finds a dry cave. From the other side of this excavation he hears human voices. Pulling himself up to a small hole he looks into the basement of a Negro church. It is a symbol of segregation-in-Christ: the Jim Crow Christianity that offers salvation without human brotherhood. The hero's angle of vision is also symbolic. He is forever the outsider, looking at the world through a knothole in the fence. To see without being seen, to overhear without being heard, is the daily fate of a servant class. How many black maids and cooks and waiters look out upon America from this underground perspective?

Pushing deeper into the sewer, Wright's hero comes upon "a tiny nude body of a baby snagged by debris and half submerged in water." Some desperate mother has killed her child and disposed of the body in a sewer. The discarded infant is emblematic of the Negro as the unwanted child of his culture. Still more it is a symbol of what has been killed, and thrust down out of sight, in the Negro's heart. That something is newborn hope, or possibility. The child, as yet unshaped by his environment, represents potentiality. But the Negro's humanity is nipped in the bud. What-might-have-been is systematically destroyed by white oppression.

Returning to his cave he finds an iron pipe and begins to dig. Soon he is tunneling through walls into a maze of basements and cellars. Symbolically these walls represent the fixed boundaries of Negro life which he proceeds to violate. He next comes upon a peculiar scene. A human figure is stretched out on a white table, above which is suspended a glass container filled with a blood-red liquid. It is an undertaker's establishment, and it symbolizes the lethal power of the anti-Negro stereotype. These stereotypes drain the black man's blood and replace it with embalming fluid. They dehumanize him; turn him into a nonexistent thing.

Eventually Wright's outlaw-hero burglarizes a jewelry store, taking money, rings, watches, and precious stones. This criminal act gives meaning to his underground existence. It represents the element of exploit (in particular financial exploit) that is ordinarily forbidden by the whites. He also steals a typewriter, on which he laboriously spells his name: *freddaniels*. This elementary act of self-definition is an emblem of the writer's art. As in *Native Son*, criminality and art are placed in metaphorical relation. Both are forms of metaphysical revolt: in the myth, Prometheus steals the sacred fire.

The crime is followed by a fantastic sequence. Daniels returns to the cave with his loot, and undertakes a project in interior decorating. He papers the dirt walls of his den with hundred-dollar bills. He drives nails everywhere and hangs up watches and rings. He dumps out all the metal coins in heaps on the ground and strews the earth with handfuls of precious gems. Finally he hangs up a gun and cartridge belt taken from a night watchman, and a bloody meat cleaver stolen from a butcher shop.

Wright's hero has perceived, in short, the absurdity at the heart of white civilization. Once you grasp the joke, once you perceive Western culture as a combination jewelry store and butcher shop, you need no longer feel ashamed. By constructing this mocking symbol of the white man's most cherished values, Fred Daniels has set himself free.

From this point on the story is concerned with the hero's attempt to return to the upperworld. He wants to share his vision with the whites, disclose his underground reality, make his darkness visible. But words fail him; it is an incommunicable vision. When he first emerges from the sewer he expects to be seized by the police. Instead he is taken for a sewer workman and ignored. In desperation he approaches a Negro church where the congregation is singing a hymn: "The Lamb, the Lamb, the Lamb/Tell me again your story." The ushers take one look and toss him out.

At last he turns himself in to the police, only to discover that he has been cleared of his alleged crime. Unable to give credence to his story, and thus acknowledge his reality, the police handle matters in their own inimitable way. Pretending to believe his mad tale, they accompany him to his manhole, where they shoot him down in cold blood. This ritual murder is an emblem of American racism. Its object is the obliteration of the Negro's existential reality. For the black man is a scapegoat, and as such, an actor in someone else's drama. To prepare him for the role, his claim to an autonomous existence is ruthlessly denied.

"The Man Who Lived Underground" is an existentialist fable based on the absurdities of American Negro life. The point must be made if only to correct a misconception concerning Wright's

subsequent career. When Wright published an overtly existentialist novel in 1953, he was accused in certain quarters of abandoning his "true" subject and succumbing to an alien philosophy.
But Wright's existentialism is not a foreign graft. Long before he
met Sartre or read Camus he was working in this vein. What occurred in France was the vindication of his early intuitions.

Before closing our discussion of Wright's American period, a
few words must be said about his first book. *Uncle Tom's Children* is a collection of five novellas which conform in essence to
the pattern of the picaresque. At the center of each story is a
brutal wrong, which is, however, sanctioned by southern law or
custom. These incidents are designed to produce in the reader
a sense of moral outrage. Wright's purpose is to portray a closed
society so flagrantly unjust as to warrant the adoption of an
outlaw code. His heroes are hunted men, driven to extremities
of violence, who face the grim alternatives of flight or martyrdom.

Certain critics have claimed for *Uncle Tom's Children* a place
in the Wright canon not inferior to that of *Black Boy* and *Native Son*. It is this exaggerated claim that invites a brief com-
ment. The last two stories, "Fire and Cloud" and "Bright and
Morning Star," are crude propaganda pieces. They were written,
as Wright himself admits, for the greater glory of the Communist party. The other three are marred by melodrama. They are
action-centered, and everything is sacrificed to a certain speed
and tautness. We are clearly in the presence of a talented apprentice, but a period of seasoning is just as clearly needed before this
writer will accomplish his mature work.

Between the publication of *Black Boy* in 1945 and *The Outsider* in 1953 Wright was overtaken by the famous spiritual
crisis of the ex-Communist. This crisis is in part political, necessitating a new orientation in world affairs; in part philosophical,
necessitating a new conception of the universe; and in part psy-

chological, necessitating a new identity. In his writings of the 1950's, Wright attempts to surmount this crisis: politically by a new concern with the Third World; philosophically by a new interest in existentialism; and psychologically by adopting a new mask or persona, that of the outsider.

The work of Wright's French period consists of two distinct streams. His political concerns are expressed for the most part in four books of nonfiction. *Black Power, The Color Curtain, Pagan Spain,* and *White Man, Listen!* are a combination of travelogue, journalism, and inspired political and historical commentary.

Wright's philosophical and literary interests are pursued in three novels and a handful of short stories. *The Outsider* is the most ambitious of these efforts. It is an artistic failure, and a key to the deterioration of Wright's later style. *Savage Holiday* was written for the pulp market and need not detain us here. *The Long Dream* is a desperate attempt to rejuvenate his art by returning to his Mississippi youth. The more recent stories published in *Eight Men* all show symptoms of the curious unreality that permeates his late fiction.

The two streams converge in Wright's conception of the outsider. His new political heroes are the Westernized elite of Africa and Asia, "lonely outsiders who exist precariously on the margins of many cultures." His new fictional heroes are likewise lonely men, metaphysical rebels who exist precariously on the margins of the universe. There is thus a continuity of theme and image in Wright's French period. We shall begin with his political and historical theories, proceed to his search for an identity in *The Outsider,* and conclude by exploring the reasons for his artistic decline.

Richard Wright spent the spring and summer of 1945 on a small island in the St. Lawrence River, about fifteen miles from the city of Quebec. His immediate task was to write an introduction to *Black Metropolis* for his friend Horace Cayton. As he turned to this exhaustive study of Negro urbanization, a fruitful tension arose between his subject matter and his pastoral surroundings. Before him on the printed page were images of the Chicago ghetto that he knew so well. But just beyond the window of his study was a rural world reminiscent of his Mississippi boyhood. In this dramatic contrast of urban and rural cultures were the beginnings of a theory of history.

Quebec made a permanent impression on Wright's imagination. His first encounter with Old World values, it served him as a link to the European past. "The Province of Quebec," he writes in *White Man, Listen!*, "represents one of the few real surviving remnants of feudal culture on the American continent." What struck him was the contrast between the rural, traditional, Catholic culture of French Canada and the urban, industrial, Protestant culture of the United States. Out of these polarities he designed a conceptual model with which he might interpret contemporary history:

"Let us imagine an abstract line and at one end of this line let us imagine a simple, organic culture — call it Catholic, feudal, religious, tribal, or what you will. . . . At the opposite end of our imaginary line, let us imagine another culture, such as the one in which we live. In contrast to entity, in which the personality is swallowed up, we have a constant striving for identity. Instead of pre-individualism we have a strident individualism. Whereas French Quebec has holy days, we have holidays. Church bells toll the time of day in French Quebec; we look at our watches to see the hour."

If we listen carefully to this refrain we will recognize the central theme of *Black Boy*. Not entity but identity; not pre-individualism but individuality: this is the language of the picaresque. What is at stake for Wright in the transformation from a rural to an urban culture is freedom from the curbs and restrictions of traditional society. Everything in his Mississippi background predisposed him to repudiate tradition. For the black man was consigned, by the power of tradition, to an inferior role in southern life. Conversely, everything in his Chicago environment led him to embrace industrialism as the scourge of traditional values.

Having himself been liberated by the Great Migration, Wright sought to endow his personal history with universal meaning. When he arrived in Paris he found a culture in the throes of rapid change. France, like much of postwar Europe, was in process of discarding the remnants of her feudal past. Nor was this exclusively a European phenomenon. Everywhere that Wright traveled in Africa and Asia he saw mankind struggling to rise above an ancient, rural way of life, and to establish a foothold in the modern world. Everywhere a spiritual outlook steeped in poetry and mysticism, folklore and superstition, yielded to the forces of science and technology, rationalism, logic, and objective truth.

In the early 1950's Wright delivered a series of lectures on this theme to European audiences. Published under the title *White Man, Listen!*, these lectures contain the essence of his postwar thought. The centerpiece of the collection is an essay called "Tradition and Industrialization." Here Wright develops a capsule history of Western rationalism, an analysis of its impact on the traditional cultures of Asia and Africa, and a suggestive approach to the politics of the Third World which stresses the emergence of a Westernized elite.

Wright begins by stating his biases. He is a black man, and on that account estranged from certain Western values, namely those of racism. Nonetheless he stands before us as a child of the Enlightenment: a humanist and scientific rationalist, an incorrigibly secular and unalterably Western man. From this perspective he attacks the irrationality of medieval Christian culture. Throughout the Middle Ages, European man was wrapped in a subjective dream. As long as he pursued his mystic vision of the cosmos, so long was he prevented from dealing effectively with the external world.

The Protestant Reformation dealt a fatal blow to Western irrationality. Calvin and Luther, while preoccupied with metaphysical concerns, unwittingly created the conditions of emotional autonomy essential to scientific work. "As a result of Calvin's and Luther's heresy, man began to get a grip upon his external environment." The Reformation, however, did not go far enough. The secular philosophers of the Enlightenment were required to complete the emancipation of the Western mind. It was they who created what might be called the philosophical foundations of modern industry.

In the midst of this transition from a sacred to a secular society, Western Europe undertook a series of imperialist conquests. As European man overran the continents of Africa and Asia, "irrationalism met irrationalism." Acting in the faith that he was the agent of a cosmic power, the white man demolished or subdued all rival cultures and religious forms. While Wright condemns the predatory motives of the Europeans, he is not entirely displeased with the objective consequences: "What rivets my attention . . . is that an irrational Western world helped, unconsciously and unintentionally to be sure, to smash the irrational ties of religion and custom and tradition in Asia and Africa."

Western imperialism, despite its crimes, has made possible the rise of rational societies for the vast majority of mankind. Already beachheads of rationality have been established in the form of the Westernized elite. This elite, by virtue of its marginality, enjoys an unprecedented existential freedom. Torn from their roots in traditional or tribal cultures, these men are alienated from the values of their ancestors and eager to build industrial civilizations. "What does this mean? It means that the spirit of the Enlightenment, of the Reformation, which made Europe great, now has a chance to be extended to all mankind!"

How does Wright's analysis comport with the facts of contemporary history? One must concede at once that he has been uncommonly deceived in his choice of heroes. He hoped for much from such figures as Nkrumah, Nasser, Sukarno, and Nehru, and if he had survived another decade he might have died a disillusioned man. On the other hand, he has not mistaken the decisive issues. He predicted a bitter struggle between Nkrumah and Ashanti tribalism; Nehru and Hindu nationalism; Sukarno and Moslem orthodoxy — in short, between the forces of tradition and industrialization.

To offer a detailed critique of Wright's political ideas is beyond the scope of this essay. It will suffice to note a serious discrepancy between his intellectual system and the reality that he professes to describe. The system calls for a remorseless war upon tradition by the Asian-African elite. But on two occasions when the leaders of the Third World recorded their opinions, they did not behave according to the script. At Bandung, as Wright himself reports, the delegates approved a resolution calling for the rehabilitation of their ancient cultures and religions. At the Congress of Black Writers and Artists held at the Sorbonne in 1956, a similar resolution won the day.

How is it that these statesmen and artists cannot see, with the clarity of Richard Wright, that they must wage an implacable war against tradition? Perhaps Wright underestimates what he refers to so contemptuously as "the subjective illusions of mankind." Perhaps the Westernized elite understands, as Wright does not, the efficacy of myth and legend in providing cohesiveness, direction, and morale to a nation emerging from colonialism. It is Wright's dogmatic rationalism that blinds him to these realities. Intent on attacking tradition wherever he encounters it, he cannot concede that cultural nationalism might play a constructive role in the independence struggle.

Whatever the limitations or excesses of Wright's world view, he must be acknowledged as a major spokesman of contemporary humanism. No writer of the present century has celebrated the values of the Enlightenment on such a global scale. None has dealt more comprehensively with the momentous issues of tradition and industrialization. Wright is the principal challenger of T. S. Eliot in this regard. If Eliot has put the case for tradition at its most persuasive, Wright has been the most thoughtful partisan of modern industry as a progressive force.

Wright's grand theme has been tradition and industrialization. Linking the work of his American and French periods, these polar concepts have served to unify his art. They have been implicitly the subject of his fiction and explicitly of his expository prose. From the first they have provided him with his essential form: the pattern of the picaresque. In *The Outsider* this form is carried to its logical extremity. Wright's hero has discarded all tradition, and with it all restraint. He is a symbol of modern, industrial, and post-Christian man.

The Outsider is Richard Wright's major failure. His first novel since *Native Son*, it is his last serious attempt to employ the form as an instrument of spiritual growth. At bottom he is trying to exorcise a demon, to discover and cast out whatever bad angel led him into the totalitarian labyrinth. That demon is the will to power: it is at once the malaise of his century and the source of his personal corruption. Wright does not defeat his bad angel, for he cannot finally be honest with himself.

37

The novel has its origin in a crisis of identity, precipitated by Wright's break with the Communists and aggravated by his Parisian exile. In what voice, through what mask, from what point of view will he address us? That is the most urgent requirement of his art. In *The Outsider* he is putting to death the Richard Wright that was, destroying the Communist self of former years, and replacing it with a new persona, that of the outsider. This new identity will consist precisely of his marginality, whether conceived in cultural or cosmic terms.

Wright's new sense of self is reinforced by his readings in philosophy. In the work not only of the French existentialists, who have become his personal friends, but of Jaspers and Heidegger, Husserl and Kierkegaard, Nietzsche and Dostoevski, he finds images of man and of the modern condition that confirm his deepest intuitions. Within the ambience of existentialism he discovers new directions for his art. Themes and emotions strongly felt but dimly understood are given fuller exposition. His self-loathing, his rootlessness, his nihilism are examined for their formal possibilities. What remains is the creation of a hero.

The hero of *The Outsider* is intended as a symbol of contemporary man. His central traits are rootlessness and amorality. He is rootless because of the impact of science and technology on the ancient worlds of ritual and myth; he is amoral by virtue of the death of God. Accountable to nothing but his own desire, he is capable of all brutalities. He is a man for whom ethical laws are suspended; who acts in unrestricted freedom; who usurps, in short, the prerogatives of God. Hence his ironic name, Cross Damon, to remind us that he is possessed.

This is the moral universe of Dostoevski's novels: its central feature is gratuitous murder. Cross Damon kills four people in wanton fulfillment of his own desire. His motives are philosophical: he kills in order to assert his claim to absolute freedom.

Wright is testing the consequences of Ivan Karamazov's dictum, "If God is dead, everything is allowed." The death of God, he perceives, has precipitated a cultural crisis, bringing to the fore the elementary question "What is man?" Damon answers, in the spirit of the age, "Man is nothing in particular."

The theme of nihilism has always haunted Wright's imagination. From his early explorations of Negro nothingness and slum nothingness, he now proceeds to a fuller treatment of the theme. Cosmic nothingness, and its implications for technological society, is his present concern. If the universe is empty of a guiding intelligence, what force will restrain the Faustian urge of Western man? Power without limit or restraint is the legacy of the post-Christian era. Having stripped himself of all traditional defenses against his own will to power, modern man will move toward a new barbarism, incorporated in totalitarian political forms.

Wright's response to the nihilism of the age has been a persistent quest for enduring values. His career consists of a progression of identities, a perpetual sorting of values, a desperate search for meaning, conducted always on the edge of the abyss. Viewed in this perspective, *The Outsider* may be read as a recapitulation of the author's spiritual journey. Books I and II are concerned with Wright's identity as Negro; Books III and IV with his identity as Communist; Book V with his identity as lonely intellectual, disillusioned outsider, marginal man.

When we first meet Wright's hero he is employed as a clerk in a Chicago post office. His work consists of an absurd routine and his private life is in total disarray. He is separated from his wife and children, but obliged to contribute to their support. His teen-age mistress is pregnant, and in a desperate attempt to force him into marriage she threatens to send him to prison on a charge of statutory rape. He is heavily in debt. In short, he is trapped in an inauthentic existence, a life of *mauvaise foi*.

One evening fate presents him with a second chance. He is involved in a subway disaster in which it is supposed that he has lost his life. He seizes the occasion to disappear, to terminate his legal existence, and to escape from the web of promises and pledges in which he is ensnared. He emerges from the subway into a realm of absolute freedom. By a brutal act of will he has severed all connection with the past; his reward is an undetermined future. Viewed symbolically his freak accident represents a cultural trauma: the severing of modern man, by the forces of science and technology, from the myth-worlds of the past.

Throughout this episode, and for that matter throughout the novel, Wright emphatically denies that his hero's actions are in any way determined by his race. "Being a Negro," he assures us, "was the least important thing in his life." Yet the world that Cross Damon inhabits before his accident is a Negro world; the nothingness he flees is a Negro nothingness; the nonidentity that he resents is a Negro nonidentity. It is in fact the very world of the Chicago postal clerk that Wright describes with such obvious loathing in *Lawd Today*. In denying the racial implications of *The Outsider* he denies the basic continuity of his fiction.

The subway scene, for example, is linked in Wright's imagination to "The Man Who Lived Underground." As we have seen, he employs the underground motif as a symbol of Negro self-immolation. In effect, Cross buries his Negro past; hereafter his important ties will be with whites. Similarly with the murder of Joe Thomas, the postal clerk who recognizes Cross in a dingy hotel. Joe is a variation of the Sambo figure, the clown who embodies the self-limiting tendencies of Negro life. In order to be free, Cross must put to death his clown, or Negro self.

Cross Damon's self-hatred, Wright would have us believe, is merely the famous nausea of Jean-Paul Sartre. But in denying the racial dimension of his hero's anguish he deceives both himself and his readers. The result is a fatal emotional blockage: we are asked to experience Cross Damon's emotions abstracted from their racial source. Anxiety, self-hatred, and a sense of nothingness are the daily psychological realities of Negro life. If these emotions are examined in clinical isolation we are left with not so much a novel as a textbook in existentialist philosophy.

After the murder of Joe Thomas, Wright's hero flees to New York, where he is drawn into the orbit of the Communist party. Soon he is living in the Greenwich Village flat of a party leader, Gilbert Blount, and his wife, Eva. One night there is a bitter quarrel between Blount and his landlord, who is a racial bigot. A violent fight ensues between Communist and Fascist, and entering the room, Cross kills them both. He acts in such a way as to avert suspicion, and the police are forced to conclude they have killed each other. But Cross has been detected by a second party leader, whom he murders to protect his legal innocence.

Wright uses the long middle section of the novel to probe the wounds of his own political past. Above all he is struggling with the experience of being duped, an exceptionally painful fate for a proud man. As a result of having been deceived Wright attains a new philosophic depth. What evolves in his mind might be called the metaphysics of the disillusioned. He now realizes that it is necessary "to peel off layer after layer of pretense, uncover front after front of make-believe" in order to apprehend reality. "Modern life is a kind of confidence game."

This new perception, which represents the growing edge of Wright's art, bears a striking resemblance to the concurrent discoveries of Ralph Ellison. The dissolving shapes of reality, the figure of the confidence man, the tactic of manipulative "masking": these are the major themes of *Invisible Man*. Wright, however, is unable to consolidate these gains linguistically; his

41

ROBERT BONE

philosophical discoveries are not accompanied by an appropriate stylistic growth. Where symbolism or surrealism would best serve his emerging metaphysic, he continues to depict, in the naturalistic mode, the solid surfaces of things.

Unable to transcend the limitations of socialist realism, Wright fails equally to outgrow the polemical habits of his Communist past. There is too much soapbox oratory in *The Outsider*. As Wright's imagination falters he virtually abandons narrative for arid stretches of expository prose. A fourteen-page speech toward the end of Book IV is the measure of his novelistic failure. As in *Native Son*, ideology preempts the craft of fiction. That the ideology has changed from pro- to anti-Communist does not make it any less a betrayal of the writer's art.

Book V is dominated by images of abandonment. Isolated from the world by his criminality, Cross has managed to preserve two vital human ties. The first is with Eva Blount, whose husband he has killed, and whom he subsequently comes to love. The second is with Ely Houston, the hunchback district attorney whose gifted imagination penetrates the secret of his crimes. Now, in effect, both abandon him. Eva commits suicide when she discovers his deceptions, and Houston deprives him of his last emotional prop by setting him free. Utterly alone, Cross is shot to death by the hired gunmen of the Communist party.

Abandonment, in the imaginative universe of Richard Wright, is the psychological equivalent of Hell. He thus administers to his hero the ultimate rebuke. Cross Damon represents the Faustian urge in Western man, his desire to become God. The penalty for such a crime is damnation. Eva and Houston represent the values that might have led to his salvation. Eva is a symbol of trust and love, of promises kept and pledges honored, of the will to power willingly surrendered. Houston is a symbol of restraint, humility, and the acceptance of limits: "I'm

42

not a god and do not claim to be one, or want to be one. I curb my desires, you see?"

Together Eva and Houston are intended to bear the weight of Wright's disaffection from his hero. If the strategy succeeds, we will shift our allegiances from one value system to another. Cross Damon's moral nihilism will be discredited, while love and a sense of limits will emerge as the redeeming virtues of modern man. Such are Wright's intentions, but he fails to accomplish the necessary transfer of emotion. Eva is the weakest figure in the novel, and Houston, who is nine parts rhetoric, does not enlist our deepest sympathies. Sensing Wright's ambivalence, we withhold assent. He renounces demonism, but we suspect that the renunciation is insincere.

Nothing confirms these suspicions more than Wright's subsequent career. What has he learned of limits or of love? In *Black Power* we find him playing god to the continent of Africa, dispatching an arrogant letter of advice to Nkrumah which calls for the militarization of African life. In *White Man, Listen!*, he strikes a pose entirely worthy of Milton's Satan: "I declare unabashedly that I like and even cherish the state of abandonment, of aloneness; it does not bother me; indeed, to me it seems the natural, inevitable condition of man, and I welcome it."

When a writer can describe the atmosphere of Hell as positively bracing, he counts himself among the damned. The price exacted from the radically disoriented soul is the loss of creativity. Stagnation is thus the keynote of Wright's late career. There is much backing and filling; a desperate casting about for suitable projects; various gimmicks, stopgaps, and evasions; but no growth. His last published novel, *The Long Dream*, is a reworking of material thoroughly explored in *Black Boy*. His last few stories, collected in *Eight Men*, are promising in theme but slovenly in execution.

Comparing the work of Wright's French period with his earlier achievement, we must acknowledge a precipitous decline. To account for this decline is our concluding task. The standard explanation has been Wright's Parisian exile. In moving to France, it is argued, he cut himself off from his roots in American Negro experience. Not without a certain plausibility, this explanation ignores the fact that many American writers, including some Negroes, have done their finest work in exile. If geography is not the point, we must seek the causes of Wright's aesthetic failure in his inner life.

The symptoms of a spiritual crisis will be found above all in a writer's language. It is true that Wright's dialogue, his rendition of living speech, suffers when he moves to France. Attuned now to a foreign tongue, his ear is deadened to the cadences of Negro speech. But the disease is far more serious. There is in Wright's late manner a stilted quality, a pompousness, a lack of observation, an absence of the smells and savors and juices of existence. The style becomes grandiose, abstract. It is Wright's surrender to abstraction that betrays his spiritual sickness.

Wright suffers, no doubt, from rootlessness, but the source of that rootlessness is self-hatred. From the first, he adopts a negative attitude toward Negro life. He finds no sustaining values in the Negro past, but on the contrary equates being black with being nothing. He then proceeds to flee from that putative nothingness. Abandoning a concrete sense of time and place and circumstance, he espouses a specious and abstract universalism. He writes in *Pagan Spain*, "I have no religion in the formal sense of the word. I have no race except that which is forced upon me. I have no country except that to which I am obliged to belong. I have no traditions. I'm free."

Freedom thus conceived amounts to a process of purgation. Systematically the writer empties his consciousness of the past,

44

of tradition, of culture itself — of all that is concrete, unique, distinctive. What remains is windy abstraction and grandiose system-building. Wright's universalism leads him, in short, to abandon his experience. As a substitute he turns to ideology, which is reassuringly abstract. Or he turns to the experience of others, whether Asians, Africans, or Europeans. Or he turns from America to France. But always there is an *aversion*, a turning from his own to another, and presumably a better world.

It is a strategy inherited from the Seventh-Day Adventists of his Mississippi boyhood. Born into a world where white was right and black was nothing, they responded with a classical defense. They denied the reality of their earthly existence and turned for solace to the Promised Land. This otherworldliness, this denial of the flesh, this Platonic and Utopian strain, is the philosophical foundation of Wright's universalism. It explains his lifelong fascination with abstract systems of reality, held in defiance of experience and impervious to anything so earthy as a fact.

If Wright is unable to transcend his self-hatred, he fails equally to cope with his compulsion to rebel. This compulsion, which is Wright's demon, is the source of the violence and criminality that dominate his fiction. It is plainly rooted in his relations with his mother, who beat him so unmercifully in his boyhood. To rebel against maternal authority is to establish a sense of self, but also to risk abandonment, the loss of mother love. The problem, as neurotic as it is insoluble, is how to fulfill both needs at once: how to combine demonism with love.

This psychological dilemma is projected in Wright's major novels. It is precisely the dilemma of Bigger Thomas in the last book of *Native Son*, and of Cross Damon in the last book of *The Outsider*. Cross and Bigger have committed monstrous crimes, and the price that they must pay is the loss of love. As Max recoils in horror from Bigger, so Eva from Cross. Demonism, in

45

short, leads to the state of abandonment. Finally, Wright perceives, one must choose between the need to rebel and the need to be loved. In *Native Son*, by endorsing Bigger's existential self, he chooses demonism. In *The Outsider*, by disclaiming Cross, he chooses love.

Wright cannot, however, convincingly exorcise his demon. His sense of self is too deeply rooted in revolt. To opt for love is to give up his identity as picaresque saint, metaphysical rebel, lonely outsider. The compulsion to rebel is too firmly embedded in his personality structure: he is like a life prisoner who organizes an escape attempt that fails. In the end he embraces demonism and its consequence, abandonment. As a result, his art dries up. He understands, but cannot choose, the higher way. After such knowledge, what forgiveness?

Such is the parabola of Richard Wright's career. An impulse to cast off all servitude, including metaphysical servitude, runs its course and then subsides. What begins in self-assertion ends in self-parody. It would falsify the record, however, to dwell on Wright's defeat to the neglect of his accomplishment. He has created, out of his flight from nothingness and his compulsion to rebel, a memorable art.

"The Negro," Wright once observed, "is America's metaphor." He is the supreme example of an uprooted people, torn from a traditional culture and confronted in the new world by an existential void. This spiritual state, as our major writers will attest, is quintessentially American. Richard Wright is an artist in the American grain. His work, in a phrase he liked to quote from William James, is a celebration of "the unguaranteed existence." He will be remembered as a pioneer, an explorer of the territory ahead, a pilot on the unknown waters that the nation now must learn to sail.

46

✦ Selected Bibliography

Works of Richard Wright

BOOKS

Uncle Tom's Children. New York: Harper, 1938.
Native Son. New York: Harper, 1940.
Twelve Million Black Voices. New York: Viking, 1941.
Black Boy. New York: Harper, 1945.
The Outsider. New York: Harper, 1953.
Savage Holiday. New York: Avon, 1954.
Black Power. New York: Harper, 1954.
The Color Curtain. Cleveland and New York: World, 1956.
Pagan Spain. New York: Harper, 1957.
White Man, Listen! New York: Doubleday, 1957.
The Long Dream. New York: Doubleday, 1958.
Eight Men. Cleveland and New York: World, 1961.
Lawd Today. New York: Avon, 1963.

PRINCIPAL ESSAYS

"The Ethics of Living Jim Crow," *American Stuff: A WPA Writers' Anthology*. New York: Viking, 1937. Pp. 39–52.
"Blueprint for Negro Writing," *New Challenge*, Fall 1937, pp. 53–65.
How Bigger Was Born (pamphlet). New York: Harper, 1940. 39 pp.
"I Tried to Be a Communist," *Atlantic Monthly*, 174:61–70 (August 1944); 174:48–56 (September 1944).
"Early Days in Chicago," *Cross-Section*, edited by Edwin Seaver. New York: L. B. Fischer, 1945. Pp. 306–42.
"Introduction" to *Black Metropolis*, by Horace Cayton and St. Clair Drake. New York: Harcourt, Brace, 1945. Pp. xvii–xxxiv.

CURRENT AMERICAN REPRINTS

Black Boy. New York: Harper and Row. $.95.
Native Son. New York: Harper and Row. $.95.
The Outsider. New York: Harper and Row. $.95.

47

Uncle Tom's Children. New York: Harper and Row. $.60. New York: Signet (New American Library). $.60.

White Man, Listen! New York: Anchor (Doubleday). $.95.

Bibliography

Fabre, Michel, and Edward Margolies. In *Bulletin of Bibliography and Magazine Notes* (Boston), 24:131–33, 137 (January–April 1965). This comprehensive bibliography is also available as an appendix to the biography by Constance Webb.

Biography

Webb, Constance. *Richard Wright.* New York: G. P. Putnam's Sons, 1968.

Critical Essays

Baldwin, James. "Many Thousands Gone," in *Notes of a Native Son.* Boston: Beacon Press, 1955. Pp. 24–45.

————. "Alas, Poor Richard," in *Nobody Knows My Name.* New York: Dial Press, 1961. Pp. 181–215.

Ellison, Ralph. "Richard Wright's Blues," in *Shadow and Act.* New York: Random House, 1964. Pp. 77–94.

Hill, Herbert, ed. "Reflections on Richard Wright: A Symposium on an Exiled Native Son," in *Anger and Beyond.* New York: Harper and Row, 1966. Pp. 196–212. (Participants include Arna Bontemps, Horace Cayton, and Saunders Redding.)

Howe, Irving. "Black Boys and Native Sons," in *A World More Attractive.* New York: Horizon Press, 1963. Pp. 98–122.

Isaacs, Harold. "Five Writers and Their African Ancestry," *Phylon,* 21:254–65 (Fall 1960).

Redding, Saunders. "The Alien Land of Richard Wright," in *Soon, One Morning,* edited by Herbert Hill. New York: Knopf, 1963. Pp. 50–59.

Scott, Nathan. "Search for Beliefs: Fiction of Richard Wright," *University of Kansas City Review,* 23:19–24 (Autumn 1956); 23:131–38 (Winter 1956).